TABLE OF CONTENTS

THE BENEFIT OF TAKING A BREAK WHILE AT WORK: HEALTH, PHYSICAL AND EMOTIONAL BENEFITS

BY

HENRY E. PARKINS

1

COPYRIGHT PAGE

INTRODUCTION

In the fast-paced world of modern work, the relentless pursuit of productivity often overshadows the fundamental need for respite. "The Benefit of Taking a Break while at Work: Health, Physical, and Emotional Benefits" delves into the essential aspects of breaks, positioning them not as mere luxuries but as imperative necessities for overall well-being. As our lives become increasingly hectic, understanding the profound impact of breaks on our health, both physical and emotional, becomes paramount.

This insightful exploration navigates through the intricate web of reasons why breaks are indispensable in our daily work routines. It unpacks the multifaceted nature of breaks, shedding light on their physical, mental, and emotional benefits. By examining the intricate dance between breaks and productivity, the book elucidates how moments of respite can actually enhance our ability to tackle tasks with renewed vigor and focus.

Beyond the traditional understanding of breaks as moments of relaxation, the book uncovers the profound link between breaks and creativity. It showcases how brief respites can act as catalysts for inspiration, fostering innovative thinking and problem-solving. The narrative also underscores the transformative potential of breaks in improving overall well-being, emphasizing their role in promoting a healthier work-life balance.

Moreover, "The Benefit of Taking a Break while at Work" underscores the importance of rest and recovery, providing evidence-backed insights into how strategic breaks contribute to sustained energy levels and prevent burnout. By presenting a holistic view of breaks, the book aims to revolutionize the way we perceive these pauses in our daily grind, positioning them not as interruptions but as essential components of a thriving and sustainable professional life.

Join us on this journey of exploration as we unravel the compelling reasons why breaks are not just a momentary escape but a crucial investment in our health, creativity, and overall effectiveness in the workplace.

CHAPTER 1

THE PHYSICAL BENEFITS OF TAKING BREAKS

In our relentless pursuit of professional success, the toll on our physical health often goes unnoticed. We find ourselves tethered to desks, glued to screens, and immersed in the ceaseless demands of our work. Yet, within this fervor, lies a paradoxical truth taking breaks, far from being a luxury, is an essential investment in our physical well-being.

Reducing Stress and Improving Health

One of the primary physical benefits of taking breaks is their remarkable ability to alleviate stress. In the throes of work pressure, our bodies

11

respond with heightened cortisol levels, triggering the infamous fight-or-flight response. Frequent breaks, however, act as a counterforce, allowing our bodies to recalibrate and reduce stress levels. This, in turn, has a cascading effect on overall health, mitigating the risk of stress-related illnesses and fostering a more robust physiological foundation.

Boosting Energy and Productivity

Contrary to the common misconception that breaks hinder productivity, well-timed respites can significantly enhance our energy levels and overall work output. Stepping away from our tasks for a brief period provides our bodies with the chance to recharge, leading to improved focus, mental clarity, and sustained vigor upon return. It's not about the quantity of time spent working but the quality, and breaks play a pivotal role in optimizing our productivity.

Improving Sleep Quality

The correlation between adequate rest and overall health is undeniable. Taking breaks during the workday has been linked to improved sleep quality. By allowing our minds to disengage from work-related stressors, we create a conducive environment for better sleep patterns, ensuring that the body and mind rejuvenate during the night.

Decreasing the Risk of Chronic Diseases

Chronic diseases, often fueled by sedentary lifestyles and prolonged periods of stress, pose a significant threat to our health. Regular breaks disrupt these patterns, reducing the risk of conditions such as heart disease, diabetes, and obesity. The simple act of standing, stretching, or taking a brief walk can be a potent preventive measure against the insidious onset of chronic ailments.

Improving Cardiovascular Health

The cardiovascular system, a vital component of our physiological machinery, receives substantial benefits from taking breaks. Engaging in light physical activity during breaks promotes blood circulation, reduces blood pressure, and enhances heart health. These small, intentional pauses in our day contribute to a more resilient and responsive cardiovascular system.

Increasing Physical Fitness

Breaks need not be confined to sedentary moments of reprieve. Incorporating short bursts of physical activity during breaks can significantly contribute to our overall fitness. Whether it's a brisk walk, stretching exercises, or even a quick workout routine, these activities enhance muscle tone, flexibility, and endurance, fostering a more active and healthy lifestyle.

Improving the Immune System

A robust immune system is our body's frontline defense against illnesses. Breaks play a crucial role in supporting immune function by reducing stress, promoting relaxation, and allowing the body to allocate resources towards bolstering its defenses. As we take deliberate breaks, we fortify our immune system, creating a resilient shield against various health challenges.

CHAPTER 2

THE MENTAL BENEFITS OF TAKING BREAKS

In the relentless pursuit of professional excellence, the mind often becomes the battleground for stress, anxiety, and cognitive fatigue. Chapter 2 of "The Benefit of Taking a Break while at Work" explores the profound mental advantages that breaks offer, positioning them as essential intervals for sustaining and enhancing our cognitive prowess.

Reducing Stress and Anxiety

At the forefront of mental benefits lies the capacity of breaks to alleviate stress and anxiety. Continuous engagement in tasks

16

without respite can lead to cognitive overload, inducing a heightened state of stress. Strategic breaks act as a release valve, allowing the mind to disengage and reset. By interrupting the continuous stream of stressors, breaks become instrumental in fostering a more serene and balanced mental state.

Improving Cognitive Function and Creativity

The relationship between breaks and cognitive function is intricate and fascinating. Far from hindering productivity, well-timed respites have been shown to enhance cognitive function and creativity. Moments of mental relaxation enable the brain to consolidate information, make novel connections, and incubate creative ideas. The space created during breaks becomes a fertile ground for innovation and problem-solving.

17

Improving Focus and Concentration

Contrary to the misconception that breaks disrupt concentration, research indicates that they are pivotal in sustaining focus. Short breaks prevent mental fatigue, allowing individuals to maintain higher levels of concentration over extended periods. This deliberate intermission not only revitalizes the mind but also promotes sustained attention and higher-quality work.

Increasing Positive Emotions

Taking breaks introduces an element of joy and relaxation into the workday, fostering positive emotions. Whether it's a brief walk, social interaction, or a moment of mindfulness, these pauses contribute to an overall positive mental atmosphere. Positivity, in turn, enhances our mental resilience, making us better equipped to navigate challenges with optimism and creativity.

Reducing Negative Emotions

Continual engagement in tasks without breaks can lead to the accumulation of negative emotions, such as frustration and irritability. By providing intervals for mental reprieve, breaks interrupt the progression of negative emotions. This interruption allows individuals to approach tasks with a refreshed perspective, mitigating the impact of emotional strain on mental well-being.

Boosting Problem-Solving Skills

The ability to solve complex problems is a hallmark of cognitive agility. Breaks play a pivotal role in boosting problem-solving skills by facilitating divergent thinking. The temporary shift away from a specific problem allows the mind to subconsciously process information, leading to novel insights and innovative solutions when returning to the task at hand.

CHAPTER 3

THE EMOTIONAL BENEFITS OF TAKING BREAKS

Within the bustling landscape of professional life, emotions often take a back seat to deadlines and responsibilities. However, in Chapter 3 of "The Benefit of Taking a Break while at Work," we delve into the profound emotional advantages that breaks offer, illuminating their role in fostering a more balanced and fulfilling work experience.

Reducing Burnout and Exhaustion

Burnout, characterized by chronic workplace stress that leads to physical and emotional exhaustion, is a prevalent challenge in today's professional environment. Taking breaks emerges as a powerful antidote to burnout, providing crucial intervals for mental and emotional recuperation. These pauses act as a shield against the cumulative toll of stress, enabling individuals to return to their tasks with renewed enthusiasm and resilience.

Boosting Your Sense of Well-being

A fundamental emotional benefit of breaks is their positive impact on overall well-being. Moments of reprieve from work-related stressors contribute to a more balanced emotional state, fostering feelings of contentment and satisfaction. By acknowledging breaks as opportunities for self-care, individuals can cultivate a sense of well-being that extends beyond the immediate work context.

Enhancing Social Relationships

Breaks, often seen as opportunities for social interactions, play a pivotal role in fostering a sense of community within the workplace. Shared breaks provide valuable moments for colleagues to connect, share experiences, and build relationships. These social interactions contribute to a positive work culture, enhancing the emotional fabric of the workplace.

Improving Your Relationships with Others

The emotional benefits of breaks extend beyond the immediate work environment to influence interpersonal relationships. By providing intervals for mental and emotional rejuvenation, breaks enable individuals to approach interactions with others from a more positive and empathetic standpoint. This, in turn, contributes to the cultivation of healthier and more supportive relationships.

Increasing Your Sense of Gratitude

Taking breaks offers individuals the opportunity to step back and reflect, fostering a heightened sense of gratitude. Whether it's appreciating the natural surroundings during a walk or reflecting on positive aspects of one's life, breaks become moments of mindfulness that contribute to a more grateful and positive outlook.

Increasing Your Sense of Connection to Others

Breaks, when used intentionally, can serve as bridges to deeper connections with others. Shared activities during breaks, such as communal lunches or team-building exercises, create a sense of camaraderie and shared experience. This shared time contributes to a more profound sense of connection and unity among colleagues.

Intervals are not just pauses in work but opportunities for emotional enrichment and fulfillment in the professional sphere.

CHAPTER 4

THE SOCIAL BENEFITS OF TAKING BREAKS

In the interconnected world of the modern workplace, the significance of social dynamics cannot be overstated. Chapter 4 of "The Benefit of Taking a Break while at Work" delves into the social advantages that breaks offer, illuminating their role in nurturing a thriving and collaborative professional community.

Improving Social Interactions

One of the primary social benefits of taking breaks is their role in improving social interactions. Whether it's a shared coffee break, a brief conversation in the breakroom, or a team-building activity, these moments of respite provide fertile ground for colleagues to connect on a personal level. Such interactions contribute to a more cohesive and supportive work environment.

Increasing Your Ability to Empathize

Breaks act as catalysts for empathy by offering individuals the opportunity to step away from the immediate demands of work and connect with others on a human level. Engaging in casual conversations or shared activities during breaks fosters a deeper understanding of colleagues' perspectives and experiences, ultimately enhancing the ability to empathize.

Improving Your Communication Skills

Effective communication is the cornerstone of collaborative work environments. Breaks, by encouraging informal conversations and team-building activities, contribute to the improvement of communication skills. These moments of relaxed interaction create an environment where individuals feel more comfortable expressing ideas, opinions, and concerns.

Enhancing Your Sense of Community

The sense of community within a workplace is vital for fostering collaboration and a positive working atmosphere. Breaks provide opportunities for team members to come together outside the formalities of work tasks. Shared experiences during breaks, whether it's celebrating milestones or engaging in recreational activities, contribute to the development of a strong sense of community.

Increasing Feelings of Belonging

Taking breaks offers individuals a chance to belong and be part of a larger whole. The shared experience of taking a break, engaging in communal activities, or even participating in office traditions fosters a sense of belonging among colleagues. This sense of belonging contributes to a positive workplace culture and improves overall job satisfaction.

Helping You Build and Maintain Friendships

Breaks play a crucial role in building and maintaining friendships in the

29

workplace. Informal interactions during breaks create opportunities for colleagues to get to know each other beyond their professional roles. Whether it's grabbing lunch together or participating in team-building exercises, breaks facilitate the development of genuine friendships that can contribute to a more positive and supportive work environment.

CHAPTER 5

HOW TO TAKE BREAKS EFFECTIVELY

Understanding the importance of breaks is only the first step; the key lies in taking breaks effectively to reap their full benefits. In Chapter 5 of "The Benefit of Taking a Break while at Work," we explore practical strategies and approaches for maximizing the positive impact of breaks on health, physical well-being, and emotional balance.

Taking Short, Frequent Breaks

The traditional adage "less is more" holds true when it comes to breaks. Rather than waiting for a single, extended break, consider incorporating short, frequent breaks into your routine. These micro-pauses allow for mental and physical rejuvenation without disrupting the flow of your work. The cumulative effect of these brief respites can be remarkably beneficial for sustained energy and focus.

Taking Physically Active Breaks

Physical activity has unparalleled benefits for both the body and mind. Incorporating physically active breaks, such as a brisk walk, stretching exercises, or even a quick workout routine, can invigorate the body and combat the sedentary effects of desk-bound work. These breaks not only contribute to physical fitness but also enhance mental clarity and focus.

Taking Mentally Refreshing Breaks

Mental refreshment is a crucial aspect of effective breaks. Engage in activities that allow your mind to disengage from work-related stressors. This might include activities like mindfulness exercises, deep breathing, or simply enjoying a few moments of quiet contemplation. These breaks promote mental clarity, reduce cognitive fatigue, and prepare you for the tasks ahead.

Taking Breaks That Are Meaningful and Enjoyable

The effectiveness of breaks is heightened when they are not only purposeful but also enjoyable. Identify activities that bring you joy and meaning. Whether it's reading a book, listening to music, or pursuing a hobby, infusing your breaks with enjoyable and meaningful activities enhances their positive impact on your overall well-being.

Taking Breaks That Are Restful and Relaxing

Restful breaks are essential for combating the stresses of a demanding workday. Opt for activities that promote relaxation, such as taking a power nap, practicing progressive muscle relaxation, or engaging in a brief meditation session. These breaks offer a respite for the mind and body, allowing for a more balanced and rejuvenated state.

Taking Breaks That Are Personalized to Your Needs

There is no one-size-fits-all approach to effective breaks. Recognize and respect your individual needs and preferences. Whether you thrive on social interactions, quiet solitude, or a combination of both, tailor your breaks to align with your unique preferences. Personalizing your breaks ensures that they resonate with you on a deeper level, making them more effective and fulfilling.

CHAPTER 6

TIPS FOR MANAGING BREAKS AT WORK

Effectively managing breaks is not just about taking time off; it's about integrating moments of respite seamlessly into your workday to enhance overall well-being and productivity. In Chapter 6 of "The Benefit of Taking a Break while at Work," we explore practical tips for navigating the delicate balance between work and breaks while optimizing their impact on health, physical vitality, and emotional equilibrium.

Finding the Balance between Work and Breaks

Achieving the right balance between work and breaks is essential for sustained productivity and well-being. Striking this balance involves understanding your work rhythm, identifying optimal break intervals, and recognizing when breaks are most beneficial. It's not about the quantity of breaks but their strategic placement to complement your workflow.

Scheduling Breaks into Your Workday

Intentional scheduling of breaks transforms them from spontaneous respites into essential components of your daily routine. Incorporate dedicated break times into your work schedule to ensure regular intervals for rest and rejuvenation. Treat these breaks with the same importance as your work tasks, creating a rhythm that supports sustained focus and energy.

Taking Advantage of Work Breaks to Relax

Breaks are opportunities for relaxation, and utilizing them effectively requires intentional choices. Engage in activities that promote relaxation, such as deep breathing exercises, short walks, or mindful moments. These intentional breaks provide a mental reset, allowing you to return to work with a clearer and more focused mindset.

Using Breaks to Re-energize Yourself

Breaks should serve as moments of revitalization, not just downtime. Opt for activities that re-energize both your mind and body. Whether it's engaging in physical exercises, enjoying a nutritious snack, or incorporating a power nap, these activities can boost your energy levels and contribute to sustained productivity.

Setting Boundaries around Your Breaks

Establishing clear boundaries around your breaks is crucial for their effectiveness. Communicate your break schedule to colleagues and set expectations for uninterrupted time during these intervals. By creating a boundary between work and break time, you cultivate an environment that respects the importance of both.

Practicing Self-Care during Breaks

Breaks are opportunities for self-care, and incorporating intentional self-care practices enhances their impact. Whether it's practicing mindfulness, reading a book, or engaging in activities that bring you joy, these moments contribute to your overall well-being, creating a more balanced and resilient approach to work.

Communicating with Your Co-workers and Manager about Your Breaks

Open communication with colleagues and managers is essential for effective break management. Clearly communicate your break schedule and preferences, fostering an understanding work environment. Discussing breaks with your team ensures alignment and support, creating a workplace culture that values the importance of balance and well-being.

CHAPTER 7

THE IMPORTANCE OF SELF-CARE

Amid the demands of modern life and the often-hectic pace of the workplace, the concept of self-care emerges as a powerful and transformative practice. In Chapter 7 of "The Benefit of Taking a Break while at Work," we delve into the multifaceted importance of self-care, exploring its profound impact on mental health, physical well-being, emotional equilibrium, productivity, relationships, long-term happiness, and stress management.

The Benefits of Self-Care for Mental Health

Prioritizing self-care is a cornerstone for maintaining optimal mental

41

health. Taking intentional breaks, engaging in activities that bring joy, and incorporating moments of relaxation contribute to stress reduction and the prevention of burnout. By fostering a positive mental environment, self-care acts as a protective shield against the strains of daily life.

The Benefits of Self-Care for Physical Health

Self-care extends beyond mental well-being, profoundly impacting physical health. Regular breaks that involve physical activity, nutritious meals, and adequate rest contribute to enhanced overall health. The ripple effect of self-care on physical vitality manifests in increased energy levels, improved immune function, and a lowered risk of chronic diseases.

The Benefits of Self-Care for Emotional Well-being

Emotional well-being is intricately linked to self-care practices. Taking breaks for activities that resonate with personal enjoyment and meaning cultivates a positive emotional state. The intentional nurturing of positive emotions through self-care contributes to emotional resilience, fostering a more balanced and adaptive response to life's challenges.

The Benefits of Self-Care for Productivity

Contrary to the belief that self-care hinders productivity, it serves as a catalyst for sustained effectiveness. Regular breaks and self-care practices prevent cognitive fatigue, allowing individuals to maintain focus and creativity. The resulting boost in mental clarity and motivation positively influences overall productivity and the quality of work.

The Benefits of Self-Care for Relationships

Self-care is not a solitary endeavor; it radiates outward, influencing the quality of relationships. When individuals prioritize their well-being, they bring a more positive and balanced presence to their interactions. The ripple effect extends to personal and professional relationships, fostering a supportive and harmonious social environment.

The Benefits of Self-Care for Long-Term Happiness

The pursuit of long-term happiness finds its foundation in consistent self-care practices. By aligning daily activities with personal values and well-being, individuals create a fulfilling and purpose-driven life. The intentional cultivation of joy, satisfaction, and contentment through self-care becomes a roadmap for sustained happiness.

The Benefits of Self-Care for Stress Management

Stress management is a pivotal aspect of self-care. Breaks that include relaxation techniques, mindfulness, and activities that bring joy serve as effective stress mitigation strategies. The regular incorporation of self-care practices creates a buffer against the cumulative effects of stress, promoting resilience and well-being.

CONCLUSION

THE POWER OF BREAKS

As we bring our exploration to a close in "The Benefit of Taking a Break while at Work: Health, Physical, and Emotional Benefits," it's essential to reflect on the profound impact that breaks can have on our lives. We've uncovered a wealth of benefits physical rejuvenation, mental clarity, emotional well-being, enhanced productivity, stronger relationships, and the cultivation of long-term happiness—all encapsulated in the simple yet transformative act of taking breaks.

Summary of the Benefits of Breaks

From the physical revitalization achieved through short, frequent breaks to the cognitive boosts gained by engaging in mentally refreshing respites, we've witnessed the holistic benefits of strategic breaks. Breaks offer more than just a temporary escape; they are integral to our overall well-being, contributing to a healthier, more resilient, and vibrant life.

Long-Term Impacts of Taking Breaks

The ripple effect of taking breaks extends far beyond the immediate moments of respite. Regularly incorporating breaks into your routine results in sustained physical health, a more agile and resilient mind, enhanced emotional equilibrium, and increased overall life satisfaction. The cumulative impact over the long term transforms breaks from mere pauses to foundational pillars of a thriving and fulfilling life.

Importance of Prioritizing Breaks in Your Life

As we've explored the myriad benefits, it becomes clear that prioritizing breaks is not a luxury but a necessity. Acknowledging the importance of these intentional pauses in your daily routine is a proactive step toward prioritizing your health, fostering a positive work environment, and cultivating a life that aligns with your values and well-being.

Need for a Shift in Mindset around Breaks

The prevailing mindset that associates breaks with laziness or a hindrance to productivity requires a fundamental shift. Breaks are not interruptions but integral components of sustained performance and well-being. Embracing a new perspective one that values and prioritizes breaks is key to unlocking their transformative potential.

Call to Action for the Reader to Take Breaks

As you close this book, consider this a call to action an invitation to actively integrate breaks into your daily life. Recognize that taking breaks is not a concession but a strategic move toward a healthier, more balanced, and ultimately more successful life. Be intentional about creating space for respite in your day, and witness the positive changes unfold.

Reminder That It's Never Too Late to Start Taking Breaks

If you've found yourself entrenched in a work culture that undervalues breaks or if you've neglected this vital aspect of self-care, remember, it's never too late to start. The benefits of breaks are accessible to everyone, regardless of where you are in your career or life journey. Embrace the power of breaks and let them become catalysts for positive change.

In conclusion, the power of breaks is undeniable. They are not mere intermissions but potent tools for cultivating a life rich in health, creativity, and fulfillment. As you step away from these pages, carry with you the knowledge that breaks are not a luxury but a powerful investment in your well-being and success. It's time to embrace the transformative potential of breaks and make them an integral part of your journey toward a more balanced and vibrant life.

OTHER BOOKS BY THE AUTHOR

https://www.amazon.com/author/henryeparkins

Note Page

5............................Date................

Use this page for all writing during reading or study.

Note Page

5............................Date.................

Use this page for all writing during reading or study.

Note Page

5.........................Date................

Use this page for all writing during reading or study.

Note Page
5...........................Date................

Use this page for all writing during reading or study.

Note Page

5..........................Date................

Use this page for all writing during reading or study.

Note Page

5.........................Date................

Use this page for all writing during reading or study.

Note Page

5..........................Date................

Use this page for all writing during reading or study.

Note Page

5...........................Date................

Use this page for all writing during reading or study.

Note Page

5...........................Date.................

Use this page for all writing during reading or study.

Note Page

5...........................Date.................

Use this page for all writing during reading or study.

Note Page
5...........................Date................

Use this page for all writing during reading or study.

Note Page

5...........................Date.................

Use this page for all writing during reading or study.

Note Page

5.........................Date.................

Use this page for all writing during reading or study.

Note Page

5..........................Date................

Use this page for all writing during reading or study.

Note Page
5.........................Date................

Use this page for all writing during reading or study.

Note Page

5..........................Date.................

Use this page for all writing during reading or study.

Note Page
5..........................Date................

Use this page for all writing during reading or study.

THE BENEFIT OF TAKING A BREAK WHILE AT WORK: HEALTH, PHYSICAL AND EMOTIONAL BENEFITS

Note Page

5.........................Date................

Use this page for all writing during reading or study.

Note Page

5..........................Date................

Use this page for all writing during reading or study.

Note Page

5...........................Date................

Use this page for all writing during reading or study.

Note Page

5...........................Date.................

Use this page for all writing during reading or study.

Note Page

5.........................Date.................

Use this page for all writing during reading or study.

Note Page
5.........................Date................

Use this page for all writing during reading or study.

Note Page

5..........................Date.................

Use this page for all writing during reading or study.